# The Lollipop Man

## Diana Bentley
### Reading Consultant
### University of Reading

## Photographs by
## Chris Fairclough

# My School

The Dinner Ladies
The Lollipop Man
The School Caretaker
The School Secretary

First published in 1987 by
Wayland (Publishers) Limited
61 Western Road, Hove
East Sussex, BN3 1JD, England

© Copyright 1987 Wayland (Publishers) Limited

**British Library Cataloguing in Publication Data**
Bentley, Diana
　The lollipop man. – (My school/Diana
　Bentley)
　1. Schools – Juvenile literature
　I. Title　　II. Series
　371　　　　LA21

ISBN 0 85078 785 8

Phototypeset by
Kalligraphics Limited
Redhill, Surrey
Printed and bound by
Casterman S.A., Belgium

# Contents

| | |
|---|---|
| I am Mr Potter, a lollipop man | 8 |
| I wear a uniform to work | 10 |
| I am ready for work | 12 |
| Let me help you cross the road | 14 |
| Always walk on the pavement | 16 |
| I'll tell you when to cross | 18 |
| Learn how to cross the road | 20 |
| Remember the Green Cross Code | 22 |
| Practise the Green Cross Code | 24 |
| Cross the road with me | 26 |
| Glossary | 28 |
| Books to read | 29 |
| Index | 30 |

All the words that appear in **bold** are explained in the glossary on page 28.

# Hello, I am Mr Potter. I am a lollipop man.

My name is Mr Potter, and I am a lollipop man. I work at a school on a busy main road. I stand outside the school every morning and at the end of each school day. My job is to make sure you get across the road safely.

# Here I am getting dressed for work.

Have you ever noticed the **uniform** I wear?
If it's not raining, I wear a white coat.
When it is raining, I wear a white raincoat.
Over my coat, I put on a special jacket. It is made of **fluorescent material**. It helps people to see me.

# Now I am dressed. I am ready to help you.

I wear a special cap to work. It has a peak which keeps the sun out of my eyes. Now I am ready. I mustn't forget my lollipop. It is fluorescent like my jacket. Drivers can see it easily. When I hold it up, they stop to let you cross the road.

# You must wait for me to help you cross the road.

Even if you walk to school with your parents, you should wait for me to help you cross the road. If you are in a hurry, you could run out into the road without looking. Then you could be in an **accident**. If you cross the road with me, I will make sure you get to the other side safely.

# Stay on the pavement when you walk to school.

When you are walking to school with your friends, don't play on the pavement. You could step into the road by mistake. This is very dangerous. When you get to the school crossing, wait on the pavement. I watch for a gap in the **traffic**, and then I walk into the road.

17

# When it is safe to cross, I will signal to you.

As I step off the **kerb**, the traffic stops. When I get to the middle of the road, I hold up my lollipop and then I raise my arm. This is the signal for you to cross the road. When you are all across, I go back to the kerb and wait for some more children.

# Do you know how to cross the road with your lollipop man?

Here we are in the school playground. Does your lollipop man or lady come and talk to you? I tell the children at my school all about road safety. We practise crossing the road together. Do you know what to do? Look back at pages 16 – 19 to check.

# Do you know the Green Cross Code?

At my school, the teachers make sure all the children know the Green Cross Code. They practise in the playground. When you want to cross the road, find a place where you have a *clear* view of the traffic. Stand back on the pavement. *Look* up and down the road for cars and cyclists.

# Always practise the Green Cross Code.

While you are looking out for traffic, *listen* as well. If you are near a bend in the road, you might hear a car coming before you see it. When there is no traffic about, walk across the road. Keep looking and listening as you walk. Never run across the road. You could fall over and be run over by a car.

# Cross the road with me if you can.

If your lollipop man or lady is not on duty, remember the Green Cross Code.
1   First find a safe place to cross, then stop.
2   Stand on the pavement near the kerb.
3   Look all round for traffic and listen.
4   If traffic is coming let it pass. Look all round again.
5   When there is no traffic near, walk straight across the road.
6   Keep looking and listening for traffic while you cross.

# Glossary

**Accident**  An event which happens by mistake and can cause an injury.
**Fluorescent material**  Material which gives out light so that people can see it.
**Kerb**  The edge of the pavement.
**Traffic**  All the cars, lorries and bicycles using the roads.
**Uniform**  Special clothes which some people wear to work. Many children wear a uniform to school.

## Acknowledgements

The Green Cross Code was reproduced with the permission of the Department of Transport.

The author and publishers would like to thank the headmaster, staff and pupils of St Peter's Church of England School, Earley, Reading, Berkshire.

# Books to read

*A Day with a Teacher* by Chris Fairclough (Wayland, 1982)

*At School* by Nita and Terry Burton (Macdonald Educational, 1981)

*Going to School* by Alistair Ross (A. & C. Black, 1982)

*The Dinner Ladies* by Diana Bentley (Wayland, 1987)

*The School Caretaker* by Diana Bentley (Wayland, 1987)

*The School Secretary* by Diana Bentley (Wayland, 1987)

*The Teacher* by Anne Stewart (Hamish Hamilton, 1986)

# Index

accident 15, 28

cap 13
cars 22, 25
coat 11
cyclists 22

dangerous 17
drivers 13

fluorescent material 11, 28
friends 17

Green Cross Code 22, 24

jacket 11, 13

kerb 18, 28

lollipop 13, 18

mistake 17

parents 15
pavement 16, 17, 22
playground 21, 22

road safety 21
raincoat 11

school crossing 17

teachers 22
traffic 17, 18, 22, 25, 28

uniform 11, 28